FRONT LINE PROBLEM SOLVING

---

*Tried and Tested Problem Solving Guide from the
Front Line of Business*

FRASER WILKINSON

Publisher: Shine the Light Publishing

Baytree House, Sea View Place, Llantwit Major, Vale of Glamorgan, United Kingdom, CF611TF

ISBN 978-0-9935858-1-4

To find out more about help with training or consultancy contact:

fraser.wilkinson@btinternet.com

Linked in

Tel: +44 (0)07840529668 or +44 (0)1446 793154

Why I Wrote the Book

When you work in the area of Operational Excellence, Business Excellence, Continuous Improvement, Lean or any of the other labels we give to making businesses better you are continually asked about problem solving. Even amongst fellow professionals there is a huge variation in the capability to solve problems.

Throughout my career, I have been trained in so many different problem-solving methods from Six Sigma and Kepner-Tregoe to A3 Thinking and the 7 Quality Tools that it becomes a bit confusing to explain to others how it all fits together. So I wrote this guide originally to help my fellow Business Excellence professional make sense of the plethora of methodologies, tools and training courses on offer throughout a large multi-national organization. And now I'd like to share the guide with you: Problem Solvers of the World.

My greatest learning over the last fifteen years has been that the methodologies and tools are just a means of teaching *critical thinking*. It is not necessary to always slavishly follow the methods when you have *mastered* them but it is necessary to think about each problem in its own right and apply the *principles* of problem solving at any point in your journey.

The world needs better problem solvers and problem solving is not easy. Each problem will have its own unique set of circumstances and conditions and each will require a unique approach. If you can be both methodical and flexible at the same time then you are on the way to becoming an expert problem solver. I hope that in some small way this book helps you to steer your way through the often-complex world of problem solving in business.

CONTENTS

1. Cut to the Chase

Can we distill the collected wisdom and experience of myriad problem solvers into one page? Probably not, but if you want the condensed version here goes:

The Ten Golden Rules of Problem Solving

1. Use a recognized method, even if you don't tell people you are

2. Find out why this problem is important for the business

3. Find out who considers it a problem and who will support working on it

4. Talk to the Customer and find out what they want and what they need

5. Find out what the process needs to deliver now and in the future

6. Map the process with the right people at the point of activity

7. Gather and organize facts and plot the data as many ways as you can

8. Form a team and get to root cause: then verify

9. Use every available resource to develop countermeasures, and then pilot

10. Do the hard yards and close the project off with robust controls

I don't believe in short-cuts when it comes to learning but if the Ten Golden Rules have whetted your appetite then read on.

2. How to use the guide

I am assuming that anyone who is reading this guide is already convinced that problem solving is a fundamental part of continuous improvement and that continuous improvement is what keeps organizations alive and well. Of course there are examples of organizations that have been committed to problem solving but have still failed. Problem solving itself is not sufficient for survival but it will be a high priority in organizations that achieve sustained success.

Most people will want to know if there is a standard way of solving problems in any organization they work in and the answer is probably yes and no. Even if we were to make a standard everywhere there would be a huge amount of variation in the actual tools and techniques applied. The best we can do is offer five methodologies that have been proven in many industries and many settings to work. Those are A3 Thinking, Practical Problem Solving, DMAIC, Six Sigma and 8D. Just for clarity these are methodologies and not tools and techniques. In other words, they describe a set of steps to be followed in a broadly linear way. Within these steps there are some standard tools and techniques that are recommended but many others can also be applied.

The guide is not exhaustive, so use it to remind you of the basic problem solving steps and some of the tools and techniques you can apply at each stage. There is also a discussion on diagnostic techniques that are used to highlight and prioritize problems. Many of the tools and techniques are about helping to analyze the current state but without action these alone won't change anything. Difficulty arises in choosing which problems to work on and which countermeasures to implement when the overall *ideal state* has not been defined. For example in Toyota the overriding 'true north' is always the creation of single piece flow. This make-one-sell-one idea is a simple but powerful concept and makes decision making far easier as all improvements should contribute to moving the organization towards this ideal state. Do you have such a 'true north' in your organization?

Although the methods are universally applicable, certain tools and techniques work better in particular situations than others so the guide attempts to categorize the most common problems we face and suggest tools that are applicable for each.

Finally there are the sources of help you can draw on when faced with either leading problem solving or helping others with their problem solving.

3. Introduction

This is a guide for problem solvers by problem solvers. Many of the best problem solvers I have worked with have contributed to it but no one person can know all there is to know about any subject. Many of you will have experience from both within and outside of your current organization so why not share those with the people who make the standards in your place of work. If they are truly open minded then they'll learn from you as well. And if it's you that makes the standards there will always be other viewpoints to learn from. Don't forget that we all have personality types that have biases for looking at problems in different ways. That's the beauty of solving problems in teams. Never problem solve alone.

There are innumerable problem solving methods, courses, books and guides already out there so why do we need another one? In most organizations there are lots of approaches people use to solve problems but I bet that you struggle to see the ones taught and promoted being deployed as widely and as regularly as you would expect. That's not to say that problems aren't being 'solved' but are they being solved in the most efficient, effective and sustainable way? Standardization of problem solving is a worthy goal but it is only a means to an end. The end is to develop master problem solvers who can teach others and so create a self-sustaining culture of problem solving.

This guide is designed for anyone needing some help in deciding the best way to approach a problem from a practical viewpoint. Not all problems need to have a super-structured methodology applied but, armed with some killer questions you should be able to decide the most pragmatic way forward. Sometimes it's about knowing the right tools to help at a specific point in the problem solving process or being able to diagnose which problems need to be worked on first.

Experienced problem solvers often have a preferred approach they use and modify it to fit the nature of the problem but they can still miss or give scant attention to vital stages if they don't have a reference point. Whatever stage you're at in your problem solving career if you are asked to work on a particular problem then it's a good idea to have a method to follow and be able to take a team on the journey with you.

4. So What is a Problem?

$\approx$

It may seem too obvious a question but, when you ask enough people to answer that question you soon realize that it's not so straight forward. Let's start with a simple definition:

Problem = A perceived gap between the existing state and a desired state, or a deviation from a norm, standard, or status quo.

Although many problems turn out to have several possible countermeasures (the means to close the gap or correct the deviation), difficulties arise where such means are either not obvious or are not immediately available.

Determining exactly what a problem is can be a major hurdle in itself but, it's vital to define a problem well before you start to look for countermeasures. In the above definition the deviation will likely be different depending on where you sit in the organization. Firstly a problem has to have someone think it's a problem and depending on where you are the problem will look different. Managers, trades unions, employees and contractors will all have a valid view on what the 'real' problem is. A solution for one group may not be a solution for the other groups. Think about how often you have to convince others that the problem is worth working on. If you can't convince the movers and shakers in the process that there is a problem you are unlikely to be able to do much about it.

Who do you need to convince that the problem is important and why?

Very often our problems derive from a need to achieve a desired state such as the goals in an Annual Plan or the Strategic Plan. Or they may be repeat failures in a process that mean we have added cost and time or they may destroy value by disappointing the Customer. It's always a good idea to start with the Customer (internal or external) in mind. What perceived gaps do they see?

Does the Customer directly feel the effect of this problem?

Some problems are large, complex, cross functional and often international in scale and these will require breaking down into more manageable work streams with clear boundaries and scope but, at some point in the analysis, you will need to get to an actionable level to be able to make a change. This is true for all problems and the key is to be able to link the cause and effect chain from the actions you intend to take to the problem statement. So unless you have a well-defined problem statement it will be difficult to make the right choices to affect the outcome. Somebody will need to agree on the problem statement and that is usually the sponsor or initiator of the work.

Know exactly what problem you are expected to solve and why it's important.

Often when we are given a problem to solve the person asking us is not an expert problem definer so that role comes down to you. It's no good complaining at review time (or appraisal time) if you have solved the wrong problem or the wrong part of the problem. After initial study of the problem and how it breaks down and is quantified you will need to go back to that person and agree what you can deliver. If you start to tackle all aspects of a problem and all root causes at the same time it's likely you will be overwhelmed. Agree with your sponsor if you need more resources or time or if they need to recalibrate their expectations. So every problem should be defined as a *Gap*. This Gap must be quantifiable and it must describe both a *subject* and a *deviation*. In other words what are we interested in and what is the gap between present or desired performance.

A Problem = Gap (Subject + Deviation)

A Note on Problem Definition

If you are given a problem statement or if you are giving someone else a problem statement it is vital that you spend some time on questioning if it clearly articulates what will be worked on when you part company. Many hours and days could be lost working on the wrong thing or coming up with a countermeasure that doesn't give the optimal benefit to the organization. Continual, short reviews between problem solvers and champions can help prevent this.

Many problem statements actually contain what the author would like the answer to be. Be on the lookout for problem statements that are actually countermeasures. Always ask what the objective is. What are we ultimately trying to achieve by closing this gap? What does the process or product we are working on need to achieve for the customer or the organization? A lawnmower company formed a team to look at how to 'improve market share'. After many months of wrestling with this problem it became clear that the problem was really about giving customers the most effective and efficient means of maintaining lawns. From this was born the concept of using a cord rather than a blade to cut the grass. A new product family was born.

A Continuous Improvement model

You may have seen something similar to this model previously. There can only be so many models. The important point to make with this one is that if you don't have the type of Daily Management approach discussed later, your problem solving is likely to have little long term effect. Left unattended processes tend to deteriorate. Daily Management is the constant attendance to process performance.

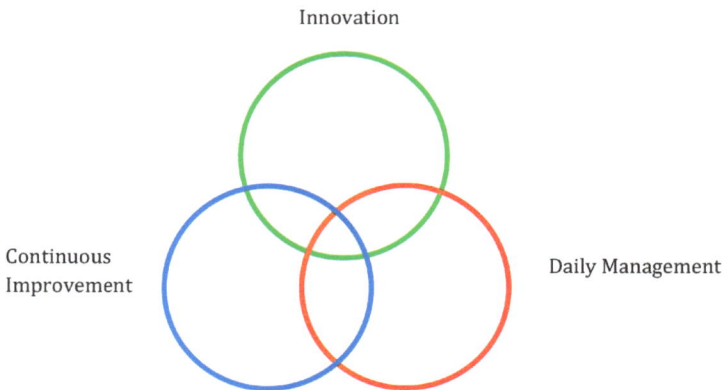

Innovation

Continuous
Improvement

Daily Management

5. Problem Solving verses Striving towards a Target Condition

〜

There are three equally important aspects to continuous improvement that should be made clear at this point. Problem Solving is about looking backwards and investigating direct, proven root cause to get back to a level of previously demonstrated performance, whereas, striving for a Target Condition means you don't yet know how to achieve that condition and you need to identify the obstacles that could prevent you from reaching that target condition. The only way to get there is through experimentation, iteration and pushing the boundary of our knowledge using the scientific approach. The third aspect is about reducing the variation in a process. All three overlap to some extent but they may require subtlety different approaches.

Gap: High level of variation (Standard Deviation)
Common cause problem solving

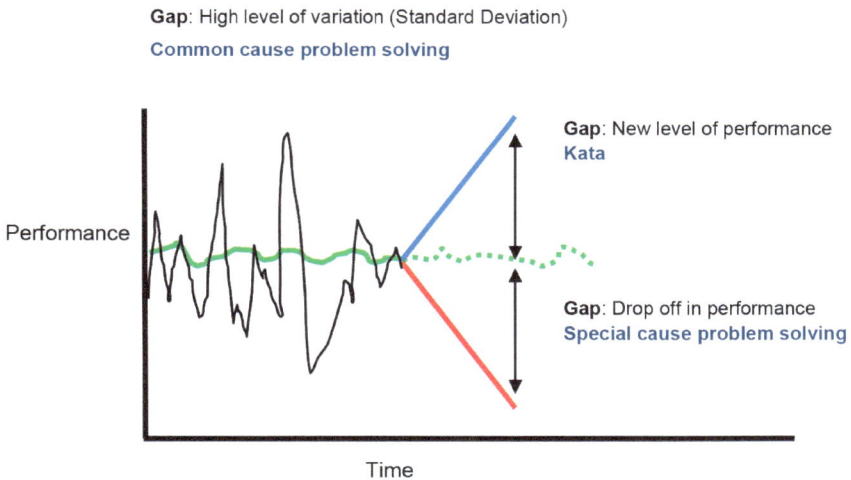

Gap: New level of performance
Kata

Performance

Gap: Drop off in performance
Special cause problem solving

Time

Reaching a New Level of Performance

Analysis of past failures to achieve a previous level of performance may take you some way to closing the new performance level gap but, if the target is so far above even the best single point of performance (hourly, daily weekly records) you will need to be creative and conduct experimentation by changing one factor at a time. Toyota calls this Kata. Kata is a routine that you practice in martial arts and the same applies to problem solving. Kata is the constant repetition of the problem solving approach under the guidance of a Sensei or master. The main focus is to rapidly change only one thing and immediately check results. Don't produce a long list of to-do's because once you have changed something the starting condition has also changed and future planned changes may be redundant.

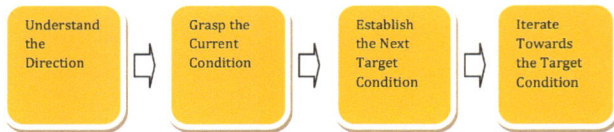

Understand the Direction	⇨	Grasp the Current Condition	⇨	Establish the Next Target Condition	⇨	Iterate Towards the Target Condition

What Target Should I set?

This question always generates a lot of heated debate. If we are told to be aspirational, to "reach for the stars and you'll get the moon" are we in danger of over-promising or putting too much pressure on our teams? If we are too conservative we are accused of lacking vision, of not taking enough risks or, more cynically, of under-promising and overachieving to make ourselves look good at the end of year appraisals. So how should you go about setting targets?

One way of putting some science behind target setting is to look at benchmarking. This means you take a look at how other parts of your organization or other organizations compare to your key performance measures. Some measures will be quite universal such as employee turnover or sickness-absence and others will require a more interpretive approach. An objection to external benchmarking often heard is that the **World Benchmark** is not directly comparable to your process due to different plant, or location or a host of other reasons. Of course this is true but, what we should be able to do is explain what we would have to do to reach that benchmark and close the gap. How much is due to aging plant, how much is due to location how much of the gap can be closed by process optimization and how much by investment or new products?

If the survival of the organization is dependent on beating that benchmark then I'd like know what we have to do to get there. When Toyota created the Lexus brand they knew they had to be better than the best in the luxury car market to gain any foothold. They benchmarked the best luxury cars in terms of top speed, fuel consumption, noise, aerodynamics and weight and set out to build a car that would set a new standard in each. At first it looked impossible and in the end required machining of engine components to a tolerance never before seen in mass produced vehicles. A year after launch they had the best-selling luxury car in the United States.

If you can't get hold of benchmarking data or you are the World Benchmark then conduct internal benchmarking. What was your best week, month or quarter? If variability is low then multiply a weekly best by fifty two to set a new yearly target. If variability is high use a quarterly best and multiply by four.

External Benchmarking

Industry specific – same industry, best competitor
World benchmark – similar process
Are actual trends divergent or convergent with benchmarks?

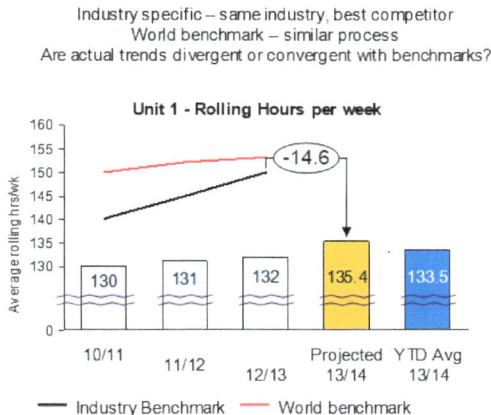

Unit 1 - Rolling Hours per week

Internal Benchmarking

Use best day, week, month or quarter to set benchmark
Use if this process is the world benchmark or if no benchmarking data is available

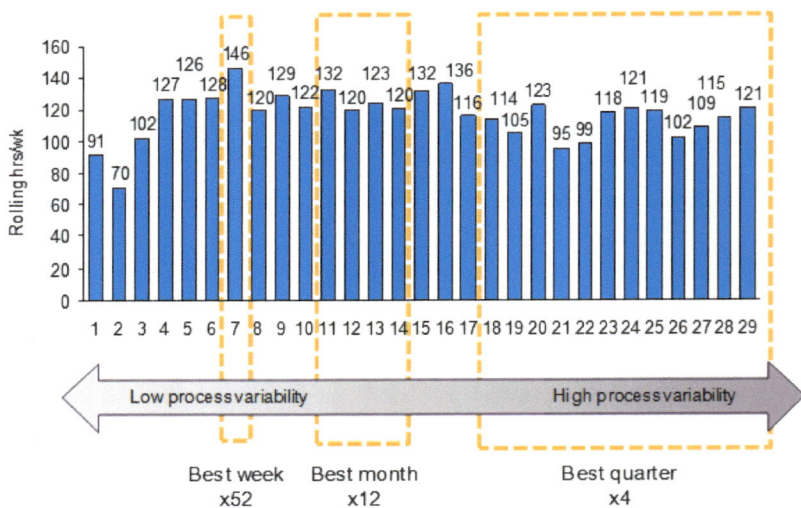

6. Classic Problem Solving Methods

Not all problems need a strict methodology to follow. In the hands of an experienced practitioner the way forward may be obvious or there may be a simple step that's been missed or not deployed correctly. However, the advantages of a business using a defined method are many.

- Provides a framework and a roadmap to gauge progress

- Is repeatable and can be taught

- Provides a common language

- Provides a checklist to prevent skipping of critical steps

- Allows you to improve how you improve.

Within business the most common methodologies follow the *Plan, Do, Check, Act (PDCA)* cycle. PDCA is more of a concept to be understood than a methodology to follow which is why the steps have been adapted and fleshed out in methods like A3 Thinking and the DMAIC (Define, Measure, Analyze, Improve & Control) process and the Six Sigma toolset. The PDCA cycle can be traced back to Walter Shewhart and later Edward Deming who modified the cycle to replace Check with Study (PDSA). The place to start is often not with Plan but with Study. This study phase is what distinguishes systematic problem solving from those other forms that might entail instinct, gut feeling, intuition, experience, prior knowledge or trial and error. These are of course problem solving approaches in their own right and if you should wish to base your continuous improvement strategy entirely around these I wish you luck.

The methods we shall look at here follow what's known as the *scientific method* of problem solving. The aim is to get to the *root cause* of problems and prove with data the cause-and-effect mechanism that links the root cause to the desired outcome. The level of sophistication in providing statistical proof of the outcome will be dictated by the consequences of getting it wrong. If you are dealing with life threatening changes to a medical device, medicine or safety critical system in an oil refinery then you want to be very confident you actually understand what inputs you need to control the outputs. In these cases the rigor of Six Sigma becomes even more important. This could also be the case when customer critical quality becomes a problem.

A3 Thinking

A3 Thinking should be the starting point for any problem solving activity that needs to have some understanding of root cause before being able to propose countermeasures. A3 Thinking does not exclude any other problem solving methods or tools but it is a means of providing a structured approach to aid a problem solver and more importantly to aid in the learning of how to solve problems more effectively and efficiently. Even if another method is chosen after the initial analysis the A3 can be used to summarize and share learning's.

A3 Thinking is a well-known method of problem solving that is used in Toyota as a means of formalizing the scientific method. It consists of seven or eight distinct steps that lead the problem solver to answer a set of questions. These questions are designed to lead the problem solver to uncover information and data that will contextualize and prioritize the problem before moving onto understanding the root cause of problems. Only then can we start to formulate countermeasures. In A3 Thinking the term *countermeasure* is used instead of *solution*. The reason being that a 'countermeasure' suggests a temporary fix and a 'solution' a permanent one. Although a minor semantic difference the subtlety of the thinking reflects a mindset that does not accept a static view but, one where everything can be further improved.

There are a set of questions to be asked at each of the stages in A3 to help with the problem solving process and these are included in the appendices. More than just a problem solving method, the A3 approach can also facilitate a mentoring relationship between an experienced problem solver and a novice if used during regular problem reviews. The mentor's role is to guide the novice to uncover the most meaningful information to help solve the problem without directly suggesting answers. Whatever level you are at, if you can get yourself a good mentor it will sharpen up your skills.

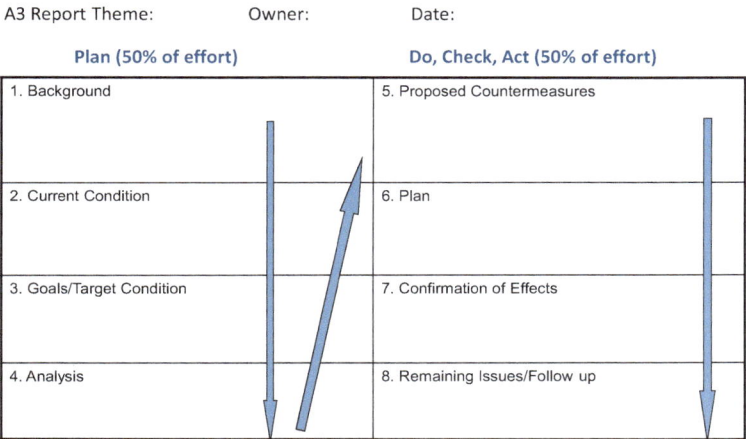

A3 Report Theme: Owner: Date:

Plan (50% of effort)	**Do, Check, Act (50% of effort)**
1. Background	5. Proposed Countermeasures
2. Current Condition	6. Plan
3. Goals/Target Condition	7. Confirmation of Effects
4. Analysis	8. Remaining Issues/Follow up

The report reflects the philosophy followed at Toyota that at least *half the effort* (if not more) should be put into proper *understanding of the situation-* that is *left-hand side of the A3*.

We can also view problem solving as narrowing down the focus of activity to a more easily actionable level. All too often we try and solve every part of a problem at the same time or we keep adding to the list of problems to be solved as we learn more. This is called *Scope Creep* and it can easily distract or overburden the problem solver. Try to solve one specific issue at a time.

A3 Problem Solving Funnel

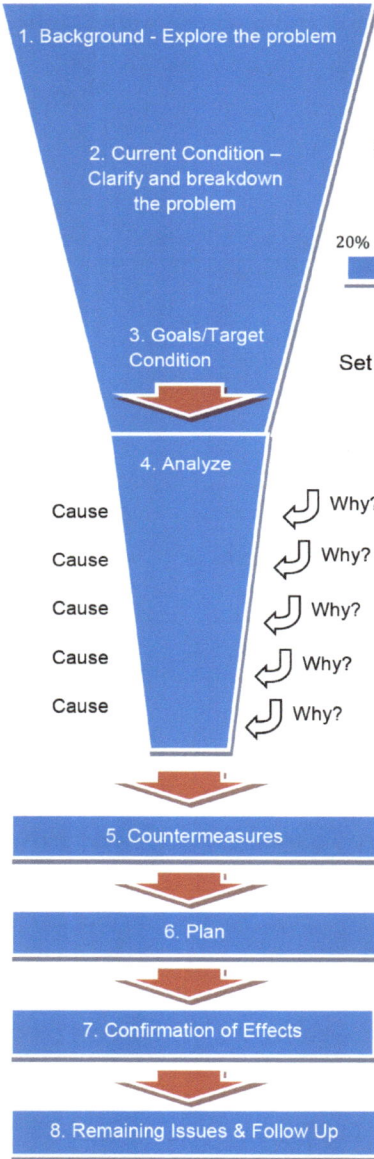

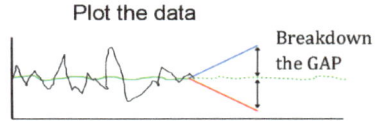

Plot the data

Breakdown the GAP

Start Event Map

20%   80%

Pareto

Make a decision on what to work on first

Set a target – how much of the problem are you going to solve?

Complete Event Map/5 Why?

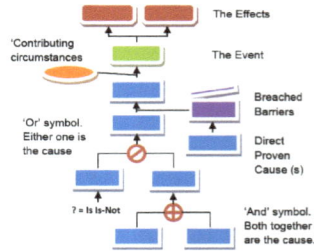

Get to root cause(s)

Countermeasures must be linked to a root cause

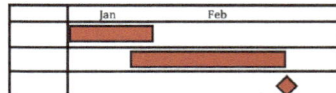

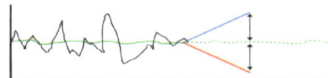

Go See/Plot the data

Sharing and Learning. What did we not do? What next?

Practical Problem Solving

Practical problem solving is a variation on A3 Thinking that describes in more detail some of the specific tools and techniques to be applied at the key steps. The first tool is a form of cause and effect mapping that focuses only on where a subject and deviation has occurred for the direct cause of a problem. It maps out the effects of the problem and the risks to the business. In many cases there are contributing circumstances that led to the problem and barriers that should have prevented the problem from escalating and these are also mapped. The emphasis is on only using facts and not speculation or considering possible causes at this stage. If we get to a point in this *Event Map* and we don't know the direct, proven cause we can move to a *Problem Analysis* tool known as *IS IS-NOT*. This is a much underrated tool in solving special cause problems or repeating special causes. By gathering facts about the *What? Where? When?* and *How much?* we build up a problem specification through which we can test possible causes. We can also look at what *changes* and *distinctions* there are between the IS and IS-NOT to help us formulate possible causes.

DMAIC (Define, Measure, Analyze, Improve, Control)

Although DMAIC is a five step approach to problem solving that is derived from the Six Sigma methodology, it deserves mention in its own right. Many of the sophisticated statistical tools in Six Sigma will only be applicable to a small number of problems. The structure of DMAIC, however, can be applied to any situation regardless of complexity. Many people find the DMAIC steps easier to follow than the steps in A3 Thinking. Whichever method you choose you will find that it is very rarely a linear process that moves smoothly from step to step in a neat and logical sequence of activities. When you have studied the problem for some time it may be that you need to go back and redefine the problem and so on.

A fuller description of the Six Sigma process and the possible tools used at each stage are given in the appendix but you can follow DMAIC with only the most basic of tools and techniques so select those that are most applicable. In summary the steps are designed to lead people through a cycle of improvement.

Define – The project's purpose and scope are defined. Background information on the process and customer is collected.

Measure – The goal of the measure phase is to focus the improvement effort by gathering information on the current situation.

Analyze – The goal of the analyze phase is to identify root cause (s) and confirm them with data.

Improve – The goal of the improve phase is to try out and implement solutions that address root causes.

Control – the goal of the control phase is to evaluate solutions and the plan and maintain the gains by standardizing the process, and outline steps for ongoing improvements including opportunities for replicating the benefits.

Six Sigma and Lean Sigma

Six Sigma refers to a quality improvement program developed by Motorola in 1982 in response to a gap in quality compared to the competition. So Six Sigma itself was the countermeasure to a large scale problem at the organizational level. All of the tools used in Six Sigma already existed in the quality improvement arena but the power was to bring them together under the DMAIC process and put the focus on distinct projects that have a significant monetary value. Over the last decade there has been a movement to incorporate lean tools and techniques into the Six Sigma syllabus.

Sigma is another term for standard deviation, a measure of variation. So Six Sigma is now associated with a defect rate of 3.4 parts per million (ppm). Motorola did achieve this on some products, but only by redesign of products and processes. More realistically a 4-5 sigma performance from an existing process is achievable or 6210 to 233 ppm.

To be able to use the full Six Sigma method requires training to **Green Belt** or **Black Belt** level, however, for those people with a good understanding of Quality Control and moderate statistical knowledge it is also possible to follow a Six Sigma approach with some guidance from a trained practitioner. In most cases you will need to identify a statistician or **Master Black Belt** to help with some of the more complex interpretation of the statistical tools. You may think statistics is devoid of controversy and debate but, if you ever get two or more statisticians in a room debating the finer points of **Statistical Process Control (SPC)** you may want to reconsider. For all practical purposes its best to refer to the **Automotive Core Tools (TS16949)** workbooks for industry leading guidance.

Just like the Lean approach, Six Sigma should start with the Customer and what is of most value to them. When you know what they want or, you think they want but they don't know it yet, you can translate these into **Critical to Quality (CtQ)** items and from there the process forces you to understand which process inputs have the most effect on these output CtQs. Once you have proved the cause and effect relationship then you standardize and control variation in the inputs and so control the variation in the outputs. The result should be a satisfied or, hopefully, delighted Customer and more efficient production process due to less waste. This is the basis of what is known as Daily Management and both are extremely complimentary. The main difference is that Six Sigma is project based and part of the step change improvement cycle, whereas Daily Management is department based and the aim is to achieve a level of basic stability in all key processes. Daily Management is a way of life not a project.

Six Sigma is an excellent way of understanding how to control common cause variation and when coupled with the more workforce focused Lean philosophy it is a very comprehensive set of improvement tools.

Daily Management

Although not strictly a problem solving methodology, **Daily Management** is designed as a countermeasure to process instability. If you try to apply Six Sigma to a process without the basic control mechanisms in place for stability you will probably end up having to go through much of the Daily Management process in any case, at least on the process being studied.

There is a ten-step process to implement Daily Management as shown below and step 10 Corrective and Preventive Actions is where our problem solving methodologies are usually applied.

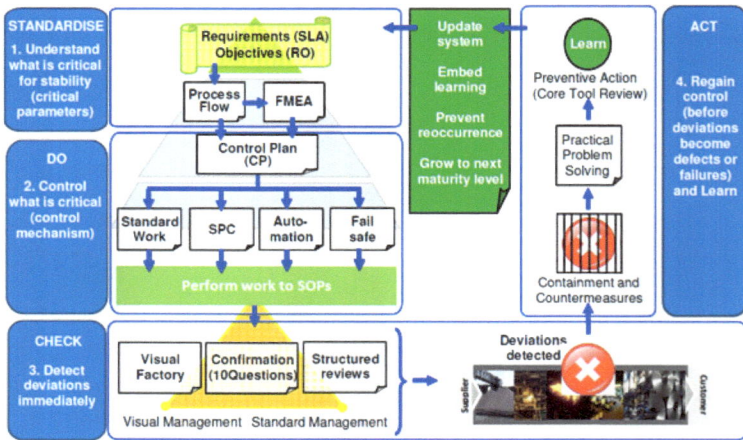

1. Assess the department against a set criteria and highlight Strengths and Opportunities for Improvement (OFIs).

2. Service Level Agreement with Customers to understand their requirements and set numerical tolerances.

3. Roles & Objectives of the department are aligned to Annual Plan/Strategic Plan.

4. Process Flow Chart identifies the process steps and the sources of variation at each step.

5. FMEA to be able to manage the potential risk to the product quality and process effectiveness.

6. Control Plan describes the routine actions, checks and monitoring required to maintain stability.

7. Control Mechanisms are applied to improve the level of control.

8. Visual Management helps keep management attention focused on the vital few.

9. Routine Management defines the regular management routines, audits and confirmation of standards required at each level.

10. Corrective & Preventive Actions is the problem solving loop when we encounter deviations.

8D – 8 Disciplines

8D is a problem solving methodology used for product and process improvement, structured into eight disciplines. It is a requirement from many automotive customers as a means of investigating complaints and quality problems. Again the tools themselves can vary but the method must be followed.

D1: Use Team Approach – Establish a small group of people with the knowledge, authority and skill to solve the problem and implement corrective actions. There must be a chosen coordinator.

D2: Describe the Problem – Describe the problem in measurable terms. Specify the internal or external customer problem by describing it in specific terms.

D3: Implement and Verify Short Term Corrective Actions – Define and implement immediate actions that will protect the customer from the problem until a permanent corrective action is implemented.

D4: Define and Verify Root Causes – Identify all potential causes, which could explain why the problem occurred. Test each potential cause against the problem description and data. Identify alternative corrective actions to eliminate root cause.

D5: *Verify Corrective Actions* – Confirm that the selected corrective actions will resolve the problem for the customer and will not cause undesirable side effects. Define other actions if necessary.

D6: *Implement Permanent Corrective Actions* – Define and implement the permanent corrective actions needed. Choose on-going controls to insure that the root cause is eliminated. Once in production, monitor the long-term effects and implement additional controls as necessary.

D7: *Prevent Recurrence* – Modify specifications, update training, review work flows, improve practices and procedures to prevent recurrence of similar problems.

D8: *Congratulate Your Team* – Recognize the collective efforts of all team members. Publicize your achievement, share knowledge.

7. Clarity on Common Terms

Sometimes it's easy to confuse people with all the terms we use when we try and offer help with problem solving. To help explain how the terms fit together the diagram below will help. So when we talk about methodologies, tools & techniques, training courses and how we deploy these in the workplace we should be clear on what we mean.

Methodologies

A3
DMAIC/Six Sigma
8D

Tools & Techniques

Cause & effect
Pareto
Stratification
etc

Problem Solving

Deployment

SWAT Team
Kaizen
QCcircles

Practical Problem Solving
Green Belt/Black Belt

Training & Development

As discussed earlier, the tools and techniques can be used in any of the methodologies and they can also be deployed in a variety of ways. So it may be that we use the DMAIC steps for rapid shop floor improvement workshops or even in Quality Circles. A five day Kaizen event can be conducted using the A3 steps. In both of these cases, for instance, you may use a Pareto to help prioritize what to work on. So you see that we should not confuse tools with methodologies or with the means of deployment.

8. Doctor I Need a Diagnosis

When you go to the doctor with a new condition you don't usually ask for an operation or a particular drug but, rather you rely on their ability to correctly diagnose the problem. You don't take your car to the garage and ask for them to use a wrench and a screwdriver. By asking you questions about the nature of the problem the doctor and the mechanic will be running through a mental (sometimes a physical one, in good garages) checklist to try and narrow down the problem and select the right tool. Of course, they don't always get it right first time and neither will you. The point is they have a framework they apply and based on their experience and knowledge they will either be confident they know the nature of the problem or they will have to do further checks. Maybe they'll take a closer look at you or the car for any clues or maybe connect the laptop to the engine management system or send you for an MRI scan before they reach for the toolbox.

So you present with a problem on cash flow in your business and you are told to cut stocks and work-in-progress but, you don't fully understand why the stocks are at that level in the first place. What policies, practices, behaviors and constraints have led to this situation? It may be that when you have the full diagnostic you discover a more pressing problem than the one you went in with.

You will need to study the problem before taking any preventative action.

It may be that the problem you are asked to work on has come out of some sort of structured analysis and it can be easily explained to you why you are working on it. If not you may want to ask about the following high level diagnostic approaches to check how your work fits into the business strategy. If it's in the Annual Plan it's a good start but you should still satisfy yourself it's the right thing to work on for the business.

Lean Diagnostics

The two main high level diagnostic approaches to be applied are *Process Mapping* and *Assessment.* Process mapping can cover any level of the business but the main diagnostic approach at a high level is either Value Stream Mapping (VSM) or Constraints Mapping.

Value Stream Mapping is a means of analyzing a complete value stream from supplier to customer (or multiples of these from raw materials to end user) to be able to understand how value flows or is stopped from flowing. The ultimate aim of Lean is to produce only what the customer wants when they want it at perfect quality. When you think about it, that means from order to make and at the customer in a shorter time than any of your competitors.

Value Stream Mapping is designed to show the information and physical flow of materials and highlight what stops this from happening in a *Current State Map*. Next you create an *Ideal State Map* and a *Future State Map* with a series of *Transition Plans* from Current to Future State usually in 30, 60 or 90 days increments. In reality VSM is a difficult thing to do meaningfully for an entire plant but easier to achieve if you concentrate on a single product type or customer. Even so it will require some expertise and the help of experienced mappers.

Probably of more relevance to a process industry is *Constraints Mapping* based on the Theory of Constraints (ToC). The theory is that every system has a constraint to making money now and in the future (which is *The Goal* if you read Goldratt's classic on the subject). The constraint could be anywhere; in the market or in the supply chain or in the manufacturing units. We typically think of constraints mapping in terms of volume and what will stop us achieving the maximum volume through the plant. Each item of plant is analyzed for its current demonstrated performance and this is compared to the desired volumes to highlight bottlenecks or future bottlenecks. This needs a thorough analysis of *Overall Equipment Effectiveness (OEE)* at each bottleneck unit. This is fine if the only aim is to get volume out the door but, not all products make a healthy margin.

More in keeping with the ToC is the idea of **Contribution per Bottleneck Minute**. If you imagine the bottleneck plant or equipment as the limiting factor in volume then you want to maximize the margin of everything that goes through the bottleneck. This requires a systems view that includes product development, marketing, sales and scheduling to achieve it. Again this will need a concerted effort by a business and some experts to help out. So in ToC you want to maximize **Throughput** (sale of high margin generating product through the bottleneck), minimize **Inventory** (the cost of all materials used in production) and minimize **Operating Expense** (the cost of everything else).

Diagnosis by Assessment can also come in many forms. A manufacturing unit or a function should have clear objectives and goals that relate to the Customer and a thorough assessment of these via a PDCA (Plan Do Check Act) process will show where performance gaps are and these should be the subject of problem solving activity. These assessments should cover Safety/People, Quality, Delivery/Volume and Cost.

You may be working on problems that have been highlighted by an audit or system assessment against set criteria such as **ISO9000**, an Organizational Health Index (OHI) or the Daily Management assessments. In these cases, if we are already in the deployment stages of a program or 'countermeasure' and there is a problem or a gap then you will need to establish if the deployment was at fault or the fundamental approach was wrong for the situation you are studying. What if the problem has already been studied sufficiently and the correct countermeasures identified. That would mean your new problem statement would be about the Gap in effective deployment.

This is all very well but, it may be obvious that you need to solve a very narrow problem with a particular outcome required. Quality from a single machine has deteriorated for no obvious reason, for instance. You don't need to have a Value Stream Map to tell you this is an issue but if there are lots of smaller problems you will need a way of prioritizing and a good way of doing this is to have the most important Customer in mind and to work on first Quality, then Delivery then Cost problems that directly affect that Customer. You should aim to never compromise a higher level objective by prioritizing a lower level one. For example, delivering defective product to make the delivery performance look better but at the expense of Quality. Safety/People first (always!) then Quality, then Delivery then Cost.

9. Categorizing Problems

❧

Certain problem solving tools and techniques are better suited to some problems than others. Although it takes experience to know which ones are likely to be of most help you should start to ask questions about the problem that will guide you in terms of which tools, if any, are required.

Sometimes problems don't need to be solved. They can be *absolved,* in which case they are ignored until such point as they are no longer a problem or the person for whom it is a problem has forgotten or has other bigger problems to contend with. Okay, so this is not the ideal case and it is not recommended as a strategy but it happens. They can be *resolved,* whereby the person considering it a problem is persuaded that it is not really a problem worth working on, for instance if they are not in command of the facts and so they perceive a problem that in reality does not exist or is far less of a problem than first thought. And finally a problem can be *dissolved,* for instance by taking away the product, customer, process, technology etc. from which the problem arises. Why waste time and effort solving problems with a technology that is soon to be replaced?

The complexity of problems

So you still think you need to use a particular method to solve a problem? Okay then, let's see if we can narrow the options down a bit. As we have said, some problems can be very complex and intractable and require huge effort to put right or they can be problems that have an obvious solution and you should just go ahead and execute. Most fit into the latter category unless you are in a position of supervision or management, in which case most of your focus will usually be required to solve the more complex problems.

Suggested order of approach

Problem hierarchy

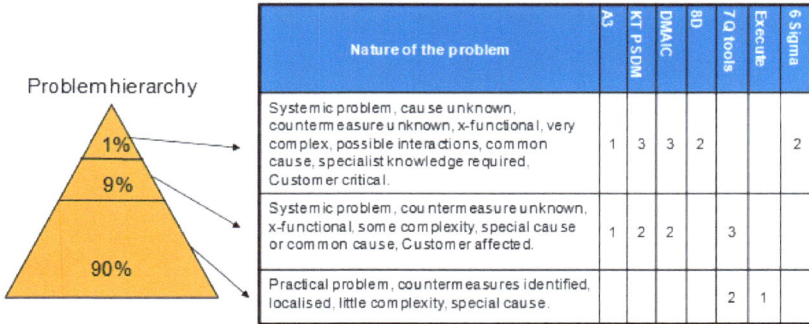

Nature of the problem	A3	KT PSDM	DMAIC	8D	7 Q tools	Execute	6 Sigma
Systemic problem, cause unknown, countermeasure unknown, x-functional, very complex, possible interactions, common cause, specialist knowledge required, Customer critical.	1	3	3	2			2
Systemic problem, countermeasure unknown, x-functional, some complexity, special cause or common cause, Customer affected.	1	2	2		3		
Practical problem, countermeasures identified, localised, little complexity, special cause.					2	1	

Note: KT PSDM refers to the Kepner-Tregoe Problem Solving and Decision Making tools and 7QC refers to the classic seven quality tools of Check Sheets (Data Collection), Pareto Diagram, Cause and Effect Diagram, Graphs and Charts (specifically Control Chart), Stratification, Histogram and Scatter Diagram.

So for the 10% of problems that don't have an obvious countermeasure identified, a problem solving methodology can help a team with doing this. The most common methods are shown in the table above and within these methods you will find hundreds of tools that can be applied to help you work through the problem.

When you are asked to pull together a team to look at a problem you are unfamiliar with, some sort of **Situation Appraisal** (part of the Kepner-Tregoe toolset) is a good starting point. This is a tool that categorizes and clarifies concerns so that a breakdown of the concerns can lead to appropriate action and ownership. In this way a governance structure can be devised and separate owners and/or teams established. It also asks how serious and how urgent the concern is relative to the others and if nothing is done will it get better or worse.

Sometimes, with cross functional problems the first thing to do is bring together the right people or stakeholders and get a common understanding of the problems from each perspective. Any form of process mapping with a team is likely to highlight that different people will have different opinions on how a process operates so it's a very valuable exercise. It's often the case that when attention is given to a problem and people are made accountable to a senior management review the problems start to have some resources allocated to them and they get worked on.

The challenge for the problem solving practitioner is to make sure that problems are taken through the full cycle of improvement and fully closed out so they won't recur when the attention inevitably moves to other areas. Actions that need to happen regularly will need some form of periodic check to ensure they are still being done. Build specific actions or standards into the *Standard Operating Practices* or *Standard Work* documents and as part of *Daily Routine Management* each Standard Work should be confirmed as being done correctly with the Operator. This is also an opportunity to ask for suggestions on improving the Standard Work. Also build any learning and actions into the *Process FMEA* and *Control Plans* to ensure that you don't solve the same problems over and over again.

In fact, the Quality Assurance professionals will always start their problem solving investigation with a look at the FMEA. The FMEA, if done correctly and with rigor, may already have highlighted how this problem could have occurred and what should have prevented it from happening.

Common cause or special cause problem?

Every problem solver needs to understand the difference between common cause and special cause variation and indeed the importance of studying variation. Each type of variation requires a different approach. If we mix up the approaches then we can potentially waste time and increase variation. A special cause is an opportunity to investigate an incident or event that is outside of the ordinary workings of a process. The aim is to eliminate all special causes to achieve process stability. With common cause variation we are interested in studying which inputs influence the outputs and by how much.

Sometimes we are asked to work on a common cause data point as if it were a special cause. So if a data point looks higher than the preceding ones we are dispatched to find out why. If this is part of common cause variation then we can only understand it by understanding the sources of natural variation in the whole process and not by investigating one point in isolation. The only reliable way to spot true special causes is to construct a **Control Chart** and use a set of rules to highlight special causes. This is **Statistical Process Control** (SPC). In fact, by tampering with the system in response to common cause data points we can actually add more variation.

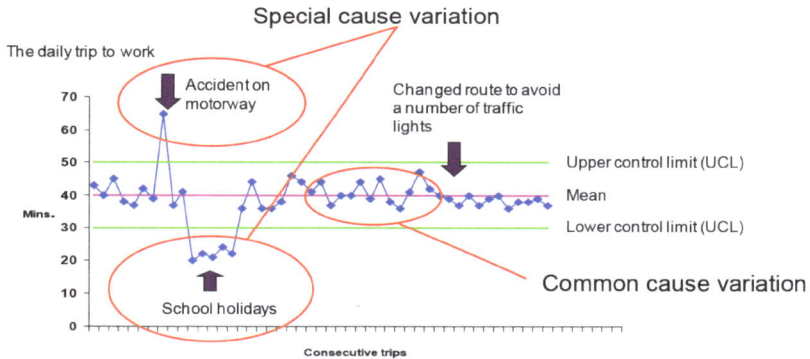

Special causes need an investigative approach such as described in Practical Problem Solving, 8D or the Problem Analysis (IS IS-NOT) tool to get to a root cause of a particular problem. If you are finding it hard to get to an obvious root cause of an incident the IS IS-NOT technique is a very powerful way of analyzing a problem.

When you have a complex process with many variable inputs such as formulating a reagent or processing steel and the root cause is proving difficult to find then some of the advanced common cause analysis tools including **Regression, Multi-Vari Analysis** and **Design of Experiment** can be used but before we get to those we should attempt to control the obvious variables such as Operator variance through **Standard Work** and **5S Workplace Organization** (Sort, Set-in-Order,

Shine, Standardize and Sustain). Common cause strategies look at optimizing all the inputs to give a desired output. It is based on the fact that to control outputs you can only control the inputs.

Many problem solving courses teach the use of fish-bone diagrams to identify what all the factors are that can affect the output. Unfortunately, they often simply use peoples' judgment, experience, preconceptions and biases to start to choose which are the most important to control. Priority is given by voting, ease-impact analysis or simply by who shouts the loudest; all in an attempt to look like a scientific process has been followed. If you really want to know how to control your process then you need to spend the time to study it comprehensively using statistical techniques.

The following brief explanation of common cause and special cause strategies is designed to illustrate the fundamental difference in approach. Although there is inevitable cross-over between the approaches they can be summed up by being either **Fact Driven** (special cause) or **Data Driven** (common cause). It may be that the IS IS-NOT analysis is inconclusive in determining the direct proven cause so we need to use one of the common cause analysis tools to help us complete the event map. We should not be limited by strictly following one or the other method and, indeed, both approaches are needed for process improvement efforts to be most effective.

Special Cause Strategy – Fact Driven

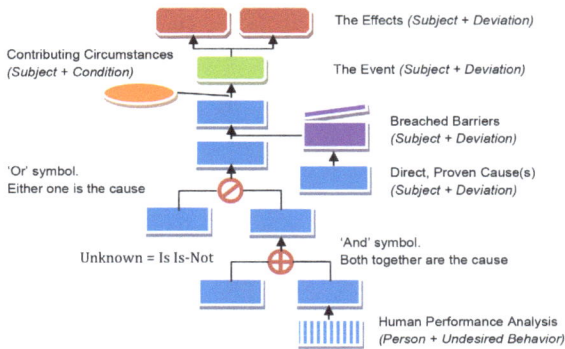

The event map is used to capture only the verified facts (subject + deviation). This may be sufficient for problem solving. Where we have an unknown cause and it is necessary to find it to take meaningful action we then move to IS-NOT analysis (the problem specification).

Once we have completed the IS IS-NOT by asking the open question s we can then start to test possible causes. Does the possible cause explain or verify (V) the IS and the IS-NOT condition? When it does not explain any of the IS-NOT conditions we can eliminate it (X) or we may need further explanations to verify (?)

Is IS-Not Analysis

	Is	Is-Not	Changes	Distinctions	Possible causes			
What?					X	X	X	V
Where?					X	?	X	V
When?					X	V	X	V
How much?					V	V	X	V
Trends?						?	X	V

Common Cause Strategy – Data driven

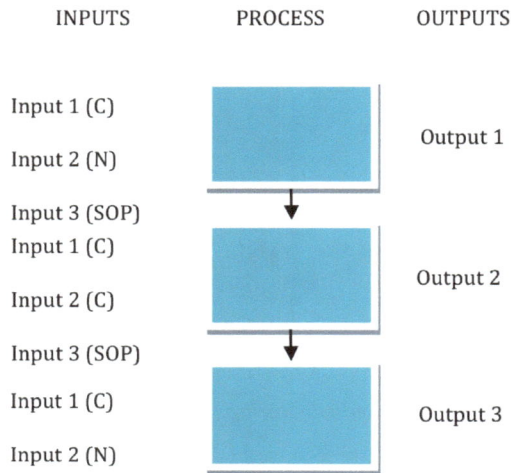

INPUTS	PROCESS	OUTPUTS

Input 1 (C)

Input 2 (N)

Output 1

Input 3 (SOP)
Input 1 (C)

Input 2 (C)

Output 2

Input 3 (SOP)

Input 1 (C)

Output 3

Input 2 (N)

In the common cause strategy we need to identify all inputs to the process at each step. Only by controlling inputs can we control outputs. Once identified, we categorise them as **Controllable** *(C),* **Noise** *(N), or* **Standard Operating Procedure** *(SOP). Controllable means we have settings we can alter (High-Med-Low, 1-10). Noise factors we can't control (Humidity, Background radiation) or we have an SOP to follow that* should *control the variable.*

We can then use statistical techniques to look for correlation between input settings and output settings if we have data. To more fully understand relationships and any interactions between inputs we can use **Design of Experiments.** *By deliberately adjusting the Controllable inputs about their maximum and minimum settings and measuring the Output we can determine which inputs most affects the outputs and by how much.*

Finally we look to turn Controllable and Noise inputs into SOPs (or controlled variables). By eliminating unnecessary variables we will create a more stable process; less tampering.

Operator Variance Focus

If the problem investigation appears to be leading to a suggestion that performance has declined or is overly variable due to manual operations then the *SDCA (Standardize, Do, Check, Act)* cycle needs to be considered.

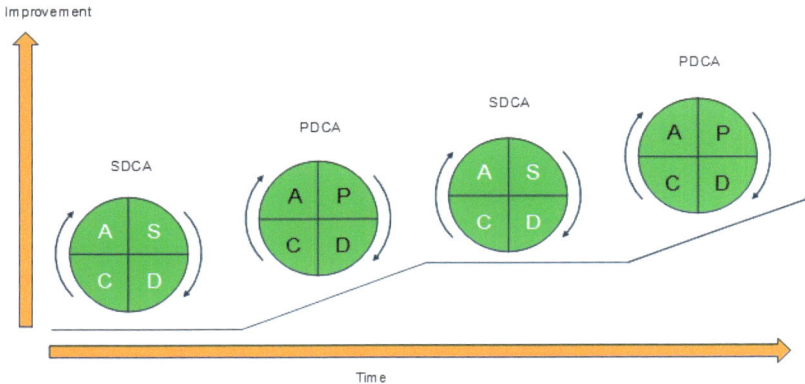

SDCA for *stability*, PDCA for *improvement* in a continual cycle

A series of questions need to be asked to get to root cause. Is there a standard? Has it been developed by or with the users? Is the standard linked to the Control Plan for the process and cause and effect linked? Is it easily understood? Does it explain why it is important to follow the standard and the effect that these standards have on the output? Has everyone been instructed in the method and verified as competent? Do people have the capacity (time) to be able to undertake the task correctly? Are regular confirmation checks conducted by management to maintain the standard?

All these questions and more can be categorized under the *Human Performance Analysis* or *Human Factors* arena. These questions and the analysis of the *Balance of Consequences* will help us determine why people behave as they do. In the case of problem solving we say that for people issues we don't look for a *Subject + Deviation* we look for a *Person + Undesired Behavior*. There are good

35

frameworks available to help conduct a systematic analysis of both the physical and mental conditions prevalent at the time of the problem.

Another phenomenon related to operator variance is shift variance. Some organizations run as many as five different shifts if they operate around the clock. Wherever I have studied the performance of shifts there is almost always a significant shift-to-shift variance sometimes as much as 30%. Image if you could make a 30% improvement just by fixing on the best operating method and sharing that.

Quality Focus

If the focus of your problem solving turns out to be on quality then a useful framework for quality improvements is to consider the three dimensions of *Variation, Complexity* and *Mistakes*. Each of the three may be interrelated and interdependent. It could be that the source of quality defects is due in the main to one of these but the likelihood is that all exist as potential causes of defects. You will need to understand the root cause of defects to be able to make a decision on what to focus on. Humans are prone to error and as a guide, 1 in 33,000 manual operations will be completed incorrectly or missed the first time. More complexity in operations opens the process up to more mistakes. Mistakes can lead to added variation and so on.

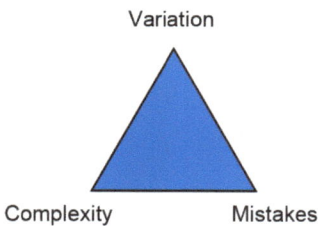

	Tools & Techniques
Variation	Daily Management SPC, Control Plans, Std Work Process confirmation 7 Quality tools TPM & OEE 5S Six Sigma / DMAIC Visual Management
Complexity	Process Activity Mapping 4 Fields Mapping Product Rationalisation
Mistakes	Event Mapping Failure Modes & Effect Analysis Error Proofing Visual Factory

Productivity Focus

Productivity can be measured in numerous ways such as output per person or output per machine per hour or output per square metre. What is usually meant by a problem with productivity is that the cost of producing the product or that stage of the production is higher than desired. So anything that adds costs directly and indirectly will need to be considered. If the requirement is to do more with less people (and get those people doing more value adding work, hopefully) then you will need to conduct an assessment of a worker's *value adding activity* verses those activities that don't add value. Look for the *7 Wastes* (Transport, Inventory, Motion, Waiting, Overproduction, Over-processing and Defects) and question if the Customer actually recognizes the activity as value.

You can start with *Process Activity Mapping* to map the flow of product to understand the value adding steps that change the form, fit or function of a product or information (in a functional setting). Once you have this you should look to eliminate and reduce the non-value adding time and so reduce the lead time on the product (improve the cash-to-cash cycle time). Next you will need to map the activities conducted by the individuals and understand the work content, again for necessary activity and unnecessary activity. If it's a very repeatable production environment then *Line Balancing* against a *TAKT time* (available time/rate of customer demand) will be needed. You will also need to map the out-of-cycle activity such as replenishing the consumables on the line or removing scrap.

In a functional environment you should start with an understanding of the demand on that function. In call center environments, for instance, as much as 50% of the demand is *Failure Demand* (see John Seddon, recommended reading). Rather than design the capacity of the function based on current demand you will need to analyze the nature of the demand. How much of the demand on people's time is due to the fact that the function has failed to provide the right level of service in the first instance or has not provided a clear enough instruction so people call back for clarification? Is demand greater at a certain time in the week? In Lean terms you need to manage the demand to smooth the work and concentrate on value added demand.

Where a service request or a production support activity passes through a number of people or departments this can be mapped using *4 Fields Mapping*. This can also be used to show the *RACI* (the person who is Responsible, Accountable, Consulted or Informed at that process step). Like Value Stream Mapping, it also measures the value adding time verses the actual time to process a transactional demand.

Service and Customer Experience Focus

This is related to the above discussion on productivity in a functional setting. There are a number of tools that can be used to gain insights into the way a paying Customer views your organization. *The Kano Model* helps to understand what features or functions are basic requirements, what are a "more-is-better" feature (more power, less electricity used, cheaper) and what might be delighters or things the customer is not asking for but you know would be a delighter. Over time delighters become basic requirements so you need to innovate just to keep up.

Voice of the Customer exercises also collect information that helps with fleshing out the Kano Model and should lead to a list of Critical to Quality (CtQ) parameters. You can then break down these CtQs into controllable and measurable factors to work on as part of the problem solving process.

Service Blueprinting is a tool that maps the Customer experience based on all the touch points you have with the Customer. They may be physical touch points such as face-to-face interactions, meetings or sending of brochures and letters or electronic through e-mail and then by phone or texts. Each touch point has a bearing on how the Customer perceives your business. You will need to map these then get feedback on each of them from customers. If possible benchmark others against your offering.

Machine Reliability Focus

Many organizations have a heavy reliance on engineering and it may be that you have specific program designed to improve reliability. If this is the case you should have tools to help with *Reliability Centered Maintenance (RCM)* and *Failure Reduction*. The RCM process is a risk based analysis of failures and potential failures and the design of preventative maintenance tasks and inspections to minimize unplanned downtime. Similarly, the Failure Reduction process uses historic data to analyze the frequency of failures and get to the root cause in order to put in place preventative actions. These approaches have been used in many safety critical industries such as aerospace, oil and gas and chemical processing. The best organizations for safety (e.g.U.S. Navy Nuclear Propulsion Program) all take a fanatical approach to identifying and acting on all deviations no matter how apparently small and insignificant. You can only do this if you have specified a best way of doing just about everything and when it's not done that way you record it even if the outcome was satisfactory. When people say that standardization is the key to improvement, that's what it means.

Total Productive Manufacturing (TPM) is a program designed to improve machine reliability through a systematic focus on the causes of breakdowns. It differs from RCM in that it seeks to bring in operators and non-engineering groups in conducting the autonomous maintenance activities of *Cleaning, Inspection, Lubrication and Tightening (CILT)* regimes to support the maintenance activities of the Engineering Departments. The failure reduction pillar of TPM uses a very useful flowchart to help with problem solving called the *Watenabe Model*, shown below. It is a standard Why Tree Analysis for failure reduction but it also has wider applicability.

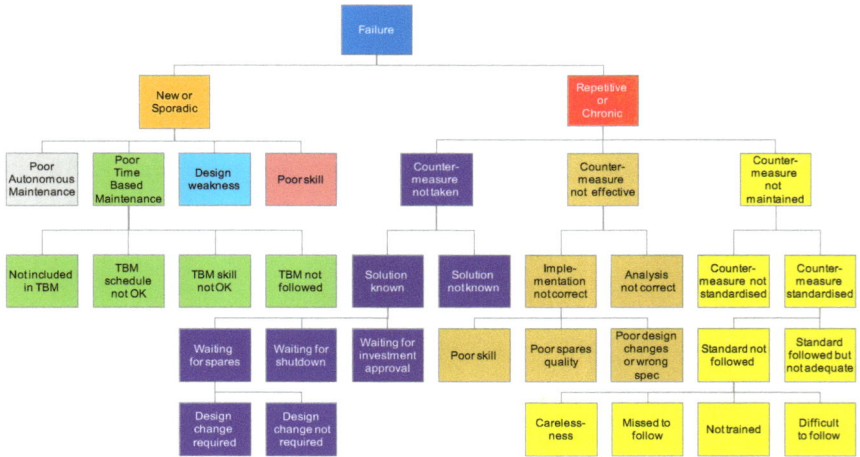

Watenabe Model

Delivery Performance Focus

Whenever a problem is stated in terms of delivery performance there are always three main pillars to investigate. Firstly the schedule has to be achievable given a proven reliability performance and secondly the schedule has to be achieved by the production units and, thirdly there has to be sufficient stock to buffer the variability. All of these can contribute to a delivery failure. Delivery performance (Delivery-On-Time-In-Full) also has a logistics element involved whereas Schedule Adherence (Right-On-Time-In-Full) is mostly about achievable schedules and reliability. In both cases, unless you are investigating a special cause there will be multiple causes of failure as these measures are a measure of almost the entire order entry and production system.

These problems usually require some specialist help but you can start by investigating how the schedule is built and on what system performance it's based (~85% of capacity). After that a *Why Tree Analysis* can be used to break down all the contributing factors and if data is available a Pareto of failure reasons can prioritize activities. Like all ongoing performance issues, regular PDCA reviews will highlight reasons why gaps in desired performance exist and these are the subject of project work to close the gaps.

We should also attempt to understand the nature of 'true demand' or the actual usage rate at the customer sites. Due to many factors, including pricing policies, order entry systems, buyer behaviors and past performance the demand we see can be distorted and lumpy but the true demand may be very stable.

If a bottleneck exists in this process then OEE should be considered and the use of quick changeover or **Single Minute Exchange of Dies (SMED)** to improve the available production time. The real purpose of SMED is not to maximize production time, however, but to allow every product to be made every day (in an ideal world) which in most case requires multiple changeovers. In this way if we have every product available every day we can satisfy true demand with minimum inventory (taking out the big batches)

Designing New Processes Focus

Make sure you know the customer requirements for this process and the nature of demand before starting to design a new process. What is the product variety and the lead time for each, how much stock to hold and where? What are the runners, repeaters and strangers? How will the product be dispatched and in what way; by customer by region by road or rail. Model the entire physical and information flows before starting a design. Can you make it scalable using smaller machines? There is a whole field of study involved in this and you will probably be asked to work closely with an Engineering Projects Department on these. Use FMEA extensively on the proposed process to uncover potential pitfalls. Sometimes it's worth using specialist Operational Research resources to make a discrete events simulation model to help with scenario planning.

Commercial Contracts (Suppliers) Focus

These contracts have both a commercial and a demand element. How much we pay for a service is negotiated based on a market rate for which there will be some benchmarking. From a diagnostics point of view the demand arena can be mapped based again on the nature of the demand. How many tonnes a week/year will need to be moved, or what needs cleaning to what standard for instance, and what creates the demand in the first place? A physical (spaghetti diagram) or schematic map can help visualize the services offered and a table produced detailing equipment, manpower, consumables and other cost drivers can sit alongside the maps. Most important is to actually visit the workplace (Go-see) and spend time where the service is delivered and talk to the people involved to get as true a picture as possible. Question each demand to see if it has a cause that can be minimized or eliminated.

Behavioral Focus

It is inevitable that there will be elements of human performance in some of our problem statements and indeed human performance itself may be the problem statement. Although it's beyond the scope of this guide to get into detail there is a useful technique called *'talking to people'* that will certainly help. If an individual or a group is suffering from a drop off in performance then there will be an underlying reason behind it just as there will be reasons behind machine failure. It may be a change of role, the retirement of a colleague, a personal tragedy or illness, a family problem or a lack of understanding of what's expected. The equation below is a simplistic but useful diagnostic. If lacking in skill, will or confidence the person is unlikely to be able to perform well and if positive and negative behavior does not elicit effective feedback then performance may decline or not attain the required level.

$$Performance = Skill \times Will \times Confidence \times Behavior \times Feedback$$

Mostly when we change a process we need people to behave in different ways and unless we instruct them well in the new process or procedure and we are explicit about what behaviors are expected we won't achieve the full benefit. There are models available that describe how best to instruct people in standard work. These are based on the *Training Within Industry (TWI)* methods developed and used as far back as World War II and adopted by the Japanese to help reconstruct their industries following that conflict.

We know that consequences drive behavior either the desired or undesired behavior. The degree to which consequences (or perceived consequences) drive our behavior depends on whether the consequences will be felt *Sooner or Later* or are *Certain or Uncertain* or *Positive or Negative* in nature. Consequences that are felt later and are uncertain with a negative nature are much weaker drivers than those felt sooner, are certain and are positive in nature, hence the focus on timely positive feedback to encourage the desired behavior.

10. Some Other Common Pitfalls

Over reliance on tools and techniques

The old saying, "If the only tool I have is a hammer every problem starts to look like a nail," is most fitting when we teach people tools and not critical thinking. Take cause and effect diagrams (fish-bones) as a case in point. These are often thought of as a good way of identifying the root cause and if we ask enough people to vote on what they think they'll invariably hit the nail on the head, so to speak. Ishikawa, who is credited with the fish-bone diagram, probably drew it up to illustrate the principle of cause and effect. So what if the real cause is on the diagram but nobody votes for it in the beauty pageant? Hopefully the other causes may be proved to be inaccurate and eventually by elimination you will get to the real cause(s). Fish-bones are useful in common cause problem solving but not so good for special cause.

So fish-bones are a good starting point but the critical thinker will be asking if we have any data to support these theories. Six Sigma talks about using both the *Process Door* and *Data Door* when you are seeking root cause. On their own they give good insights but together are more likely to pinpoint issues more quickly. Do we always observe the process before doing a cause and effect diagram?

Who do we think of as really good problem solvers? Police Detectives, Private Investigators, Journalists, Doctors, Scientists, Air Crash Investigators and your local Car Mechanic all use critical thinking to try and establish why and how an incident or phenomena occur. If you watch Police procedural dramas you can see both the process and the data door being opened. Map the timeline of events and people and combine this with forensic evidence to close the case.

Problem Solving – Basic Concepts
Data Door vs Process Door

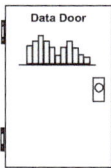

Data Door	
	Pareto
	Stratification
	Scatter Diagrams
	Control Charts
	Multi-Vari Analysis

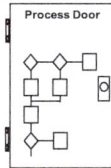

Process Door	
	Process Flow Charting
	Process Activity Mapping
	Cycle Time Analysis
	Value Stream Mapping
	Constraints Mapping
	Four fields Mapping
	Why tree analysis

* To understand the drivers of variation in the process
* To tackle quality problems and waste
* To understand the root cause of differences between outputs

* To improve the under-standing of process flow
* To tackle cycle time problems
* To identify opportunities to reduce process costs

It is recommended to go through both doors to make sure that potential causes are not overlooked.

Lack of creative thinking or artificial barriers

When you are generating countermeasures it's easy and natural to follow the thinking patterns that you use instinctively so you end up with ideas that are safe and solid but there may be an opportunity for innovation that you've missed. Get some help with creative thinking techniques.

On a similar note, we often set self-limiting barriers in terms of what is possible or we don't challenge the boundaries set by others.

Lack of systems thinking

Is the root cause of the problem and/or the countermeasure part of a much larger picture? Have you understood the whole value chain and the effects of changing the part you are working on. Local optimization could have a neutral or detrimental effect on the whole system.

Insufficient observation

If you don't visit the Gemba (the place of value creation) and Go-see for yourself you are likely to miss some important facts. A problem solver was dispatched to help with an ongoing problem of delivery performance which was being worked on by highly skills Six Sigma consultants who had forgotten to go and talk to the people involved. It turned out that someone was adding extra orders to cover for his holidays and other commitments and so the problem was dissolved.

Failure to confirm the effect and keep confirming it

Declaring victory too soon after a change has been made. There needs to be a demonstrated period of improved performance, preferably backed up with data (hypothesis tests). By building in a *Key Performance Indicator (KPI)* to the regular review process an ongoing monitoring of the performance can be set up. It is good practice to go back and check the projects you have worked on are still delivering after 3 months, 6 months, 9 months and even longer.

Insufficient control

In the hierarchy of control mechanisms available, relying on manual checks and routines is the least effective overall mechanism. In order of effectiveness we should try and deploy firstly *Error-Proofing* then *Automation/Systems Changes* then *Statistical Process Control* and then finally *Standard Work*. Having said that, Toyota try not to put too many error-proofing devices in as they can add complexity and additional maintenance.

Not learning from other similar problems or from history

Have we solved this problem in the past? Is this problem the result of an unexpected consequence of another problem solving effort? How have other departments, organizations or industries dealt with a similar problem? These are all questions to direct towards your Knowledge Management teams and knowledge management systems. The Internet offers us access to an unbelievable amount of information and it may be that somebody out there has already solved this problem.

No Data or No Facts

Without data we are just guessing. If you don't have data then you must collect it. That might mean setting up a simple tally chart or a more complex monitoring system. Gather facts, not assumptions or opinions. Always question the validity of the data and verify the facts.

11. Personal Attributes of Great Problem Solvers

⁓

We've all met those people for whom the technicality of tools and techniques becomes the focus of problem solving. Others just want to work by themselves and treat knowledge as power. Some want rigid adherence to the methodology and need every step ticked off. And then there are those who appear to know the answer before you even start on the problem solving road. We may all have met these people and more than likely we have all *been* these people at some time. So what are some of the attributes that mark out a great problem solver from the rest of us? Here are some of the key attributes:

No blame

Thinks problem not solution

Open minded

Customer focused

Collaborative and communicative with all stakeholders

Visualizes the problem with simple drawings and sketches

Asks lots of open questions

Go-see approach

Systems thinker

Gets the appropriate level of detail

Facilitates teamwork

Deals with emotions first

Has the end in mind (of the process)

Relies on facts not assumptions

Understands the interaction of people and process

Can distinguish facts, possible causes, contributing circumstances and breached barriers

Uses self-reflection and asks for feedback

The Art of Questioning

Questioning is a key skill in problem solving that is often overlooked. Right from the start you will be asking *open questions* to clarify the problem definition. In exercises on questioning it is amazing how many people resort to the use of closed questioning when problem solving. Data collected during many training courses shows that roughly two-thirds of the questions are closed questions. When closed questions are used it means that people are testing out their own theories on what is the cause of the problem before gathering the facts that will help them narrow down the possibilities.

Open questioning invites discussion and allows people to give you a rich source of facts. Using What? How? When? Where? and Why? questions is a powerful technique but not always intuitive. You need to practice this before it becomes natural. It's not that *closed questions* are wrong *per se* but they should be used for confirmation or validation of facts to make sure everyone is clear on what was said.

It is very difficult to gather facts in an organization where people fear to speak out. A blame culture encourages covering up mistakes and an avoidance of telling the truth. When we say that one of the key aspects of problem solving is *no blame* it does not mean that we don't want to find out when people have made a mistake. It means our first action is not to assume that by reprimanding someone (or worse) we have solved the problem. Even the old recourse to more training won't necessarily solve the problem long-term if the root cause is not directly linked to a lack of training.

So much of effective problem solving rests with the mindset and behaviors of the people in an organization. Most importantly, the leaders in that organization who set the tone and whose actions speak a lot louder than their words. No amount of training will ever create a culture of problem solving on its own.

12. Countermeasures

◈

O nce all the root cause analysis is completed and we are certain we understand enough about the problem to take meaningful action, we can start to consider our *proposed countermeasures*. We should start to generate a selection of possible countermeasures using the output of the analysis and the combined power of the problem solving team. At this stage we may need to call in expertise from suppliers or customers. Very often our specialist suppliers understand what countermeasures are on offer or they may know how their other customers have dealt with similar problems.

Be careful using *brainstorming* techniques as some of what is written on the subject is no longer thought valid. Whereas in the past, one of the rules of brainstorming is that we should not criticize any ideas, it is now known that you will get better results by allowing people to question how an idea may work and let everyone build on the results. All ideas should be encouraged but, they must also stand up to first contact with the enemy.

There will rarely be a single possible countermeasure to a problem so we should try and generate a range of options from the simple and inexpensive to the more complex and technology based. Each one will need to be compared in terms of its effectiveness against a set of criteria based on what the problem is trying to address. A simple *decision analysis* matrix can be used to help with this. Score the criteria in terms of importance and then rate each countermeasure against each other in its effectiveness in satisfying the criteria. Multiply each score with the criteria rating and then add all the criteria scores to give a final numerical decision.

Each countermeasure must be linked to eliminating a root cause or creating a new barrier that will stop the chain of cause and effect in the future. Countermeasures will fit into one of the following control mechanisms or a combination of these: ***Error-proofing, Automation, Statistical Process Control or Standard Work.***

	Criteria 1	Criteria 1	Criteria 1	Score
	10	6	4	
Countermeasure 1	8	7	2	130
Countermeasure 2	4	4	5	84
Countermeasure 3	7	6	8	*138*
Countermeasure 4	6	2	5	92

13. How to Find Out More about Problem Solving

⌇

This guide is designed to help people think their way through the approach to take when faced with solving or being asked to help others solve problems. It can only be a starting point as the body of knowledge on problem solving is vast. More detailed descriptions of tools and techniques are available from many sources as mentioned in the guide.

When you are helping others it's much easier to use one of the methodologies described here. If you are an experienced problem solver then you will know which tools are most suited to the problem in hand but you may still need some supporting materials to use within your team.

The best way of finding out more about problem solving, however, is to go and solve some problems with the guidance of an experienced practitioner.

I hope you have enjoyed the book and it has given you some practical pointers to help with your own problem solving exploits. Many books have been written setting out the details of the methodologies and tools mentioned in this book and my aim was never to reproduce that level of detail. If you are looking for further advice, training and/or consultancy options you can contact me directly to discuss:

Fraser Wilkinson

E-Mail: fraser.wilkinson@btinternet.com

Tel: 0044 (0)07840529668 or 0044 (0)1446793154.

14. Suggested reading

∿

As mentioned previously the subject matter on problem solving is vast but, there are some key texts that anybody interested in Continuous Improvement and Problem Solving should read.

The Lean Toolbox 4th Edition, Bicheno, John and Holweg, Matthias, 2009

The New Rational Manager, Kepner, Charles, Tregoe, Benjamin, 1997

The Goal, Goldratt, Eli, 1984

The Toyota Way, Liker, Jeffrey, 2004

Learning to See, Rother, Mike and Shook, John 1998

Creating Continuous Flow, Rother, Mike and Rick Harris, 2001

The Leader's Handbook, Scholtes, Peter,1998

Understanding A3 Thinking, Sobek, Durward and Smalley, Art, 2008

Lean Thinking (rev edn), Womack, James and Jones, Daniel, 2003

Freedom from Command and Control, Seddon, John, 2005

Managing to Learn, A3 Thinking, Shook, John, 2010

Toyota Kata, Rother, Mike, 2009

Daily Management the TQM Way, Ando, Yukihiro, Kumar, Pankaj, 2011

The Back of the Napkin, Roam, Dan, 2009

Useful links

Toyota Kata

Lean Enterprise Institute

Lean Enterprise Academy

The Art of Lean

The Team Handbook Worksheets

Gemba Academy

15. Appendix 1: Six Sigma/DMAIC & other tools related to A3 Thinking

TOOL NAME	A3 Thinking step	Phases of DMAIC in which tool is most commonly used				
		D	M	A	I	C
Affinity Diagram	1	X		X		
Brainstorming	4, 5			X	X	
Business Case	1, 2	X				
Cause-and-Effect Diagrams	4			X		
Project Charter	1	X				
Consensus	5				X	
Control Charts: Individuals (X-MR), X-Bar R, Exponentially Waited Moving Average, p, np, c, u.	4, 7		X	X	X	X
Critical to Quality (CtQ) tree	2	X				
Frequency Plot Check Sheet, Confirmation Check Sheet, Concentration Diagram	4		X	X	X	X
Data Collection Plan	4		X	X	X	X
Design of Experiments (DoE)	4			X	X	
Flow Diagrams - Process Maps	2, 4	X	X	X	X	X
Frequency Plots - Histograms	4		X	X	X	X
FMEA (Failure Mode and Effect Analysis)	4, 5		X		X	
Gage R & R (Measurement System Analysis)	4		X			
Human Performance Analysis	4			X		
Balance of Consequences	4			X		
Hypothesis tests: t-test, paired t-test, ANOVA, Chi Square	7		X			

TOOL NAME	A3 Thinking step	Phases of DMAIC in which tool is most commonly used				
		D	M	A	I	C
Kano Model	2		X			
Planning Tools – Gantt Chart	6	X			X	
Pareto Charts	2, 4		X	X	X	
Prioritization Matrix	4, 5		X		X	
Process Capability	2		X		X	
Process Sigma	2		X		X	
Regression	4			X		
Rolled Throughput Yield	2	X				
Sampling	4		X	X	X	X
Scatter Plots	4			X		
Supplier, Input, Process, Output, Customer (SIPOC)	2	X				
Stakeholder Analysis	2	X				
Standardization	5					X
Stratification	4		X	X	X	X
Stratified Frequency Plots	4			X		
Time Series Plots – Run Charts	4		X			
Voice of the Customer (VoC)	2	X				
Value Stream Mapping (VSM)	2	X		X		
Constraints Mapping – Theory of Constraints (ToC)	2	X		X		
Kepner-Tregoe Situation Appraisal	2	X				
Kepner-Tregoe Problem Analysis	4			X		

TOOL NAME	A3 Thinking step	Phases of DMAIC in which tool is most commonly used				
		D	M	A	I	C
Statistical Process Control (SPC)	4, 7		X			X
Control Plans	7					X
Standardized Work	5					X
Overall Equipment Effectiveness (OEE)	2		X			
5S Workplace Organization	5					X
Visual Management	7					X
Process Activity Mapping	4			X		
Kepner-Tregoe Incident/Event Mapping	2			X		
Error Proofing (Poke Yoke)	5					X
Line Balancing – TAKT time analysis	4			X		
Service Blueprinting	2, 4	X		X		
Reliability Centered Maintenance (RCM)	5				X	
Failure Analysis	4			X		
Why Tree Analysis and 5 Whys	4		X	X		
Watenabe Model	4			X		
4 Fields Mapping	4			X		
Single Minute Exchange of Dies (SMED)	5				X	
7 Wastes Analysis	4			X		
Responsible, Accountable, Consulted, Informed (RACI)	5					X

16. Appendix 2: The A3 Questions

Report theme:	Owner:
1. Background Why are we talking about this? Why is it a problem for the organisation? How big is the problem? What Annual plan or Strategic goals does this problem link to?	**5. Proposed Countermeasures** Are there clear countermeasures steps identified? Do the countermeasures link to the root cause of the problem? Are the countermeasures focused on the right areas? Who is responsible for doing what, by when - is 4 Whys 1 How clear? Will these action items prevent recurrence of the problem? Is the implementation order clear and reasonable? What countermeasures were considered but rejected? What was the decision making process?
2. Current Condition Is the current condition clear and logically depicted in a visual manner? What do you actually know and how do you know it? Have you gathered and verified the facts by visiting the workplace? Have you engaged other people? Are the facts of the situation clear, or are there just observations and opinions? Is the problem quantified in some manner or is it too qualitative? Is this a special cause or common cause problem?	**6. Plan** Are any key activities or steps missing? Is the implementation schedule clear and reasonable? How will the effects of implementation be verified? How will a reflection meeting be held and when? What budget or timing constraints exist? Do we have a contingency plan?
3. Goals/Targets Is there a clear goal or target? How was the target set? What, specifically, is to be accomplished? How will this goal be measured or evaluated? What will improve, by how much, and when?	**7. Confirmation of Effect** How will you measure the effectiveness of the countermeasures? Has actual performance moved in line with the goal statement? If performance has not improved, then why? What was missed? If performance is not in line with expectations was the countermeasure ineffective or the deployment of the countermeasure ineffective?
4. Analysis Did you uncover the most meaningful information to support the analysis? Did you isolate the root cause(s) of the main components of the gap? Is the analysis comprehensive at a broad level? Is the analysis detailed enough and did it probe deeply enough on the right issues? Is there evidence of proper five-whys thinking about the true cause? Has cause and effect been demonstrated or linked in some manner?	**8. Remaining issues/Follow-up** What is necessary to prevent recurrence of the problem? What remains to be accomplished? What other parts of the organisation need to be informed of this result? How will this be standardised and communicated? What documentation needs to be updated e.g. FMEA, Control Plan, Standard Work? What changes do you need to make to Daily Routine Management regimes?

17. Appendix 3: DMAIC Problem Solving Poster

About the Author

Fraser has been a CI professional for over 25 years and has worked in a diverse range of industries from aircraft maintenance, coal mining, medical devices, and consultancy and most recently in steel. In his role as a Business Excellence Manager at Tata Steel Europe, he is responsible for defining the Operational Excellence competency levels in the European operations and for delivering common training and development solutions to up-skill the ~30,000 employees across Europe. His focus is largely on the deployment of Daily Management and Practical Problem Solving. Fraser is a graduate of the Lean Enterprise Research Centre at Cardiff Business School (U.K.) where he completed the M.Sc. in Lean Operations under Professor John Bicheno in 2003 and is a certified Six Sigma Black Belt from his time at Johnson & Johnson.

Fraser began his career as an aircraft maintenance engineer with the United Kingdom Ministry of Defense where he serviced Phantom F4 and Tornado fast jets for the Royal Air Force. His aerospace career took him all over Europe where he maintained aircraft for Swissair, KLM Royal Dutch Airlines, Lufthansa, Sabena, Cargolux and Fokker before returning to the United Kingdom to take up a post for British Airways as a maintenance-planning engineer in 1993.

He entered full time further education in 1995 and completed a B.Sc. in Energy and Environmental Technology at the University of Glamorgan before being taken on by Johnson & Johnson in 1999 to help the roll out of Lean and Six Sigma under the Corporate Process Excellence umbrella. Fraser joined Tata Steel in 2006 as a Continuous Improvement Coach where he was also involved in the deployment of Behavioral Safety, Change Management and Project Management to deliver significant improvements in business performance.